you'll come back to yourself

to yourself

michaela angemeer

for oma

i feel like i
need to practice
not falling in love

table of contents

holding on

[hohl-ding on]
verb

    1. to maintain a grasp on something: hang on
    2. to await something (such as a telephone connection)
desired or requested broadly
    3. to maintain possession of or adherence to

when your breath
is hot it feels
more weighted
than you know
i am soft
but you have always been
hard and heavy
i've never been one to show
the insides of my soul first
but resistance to closeness
pulls me in for reasons
i do know
but do not like to talk about
i guess there are some things
i need to relearn
if my life is a pendulum
or we are just on swings
when you push me away
i need to learn to push back

i always cave first
it's like the hollows
inside of me
are asking you to stay

nothing is more dangerous
than a lie said with a smile

i will put you in a support group
with all the men that came before you
just know that when your throat is dry
they are not the kind to bring you water
don't count on hands holding you up
these palms are distracted and looking
for someone else to hold
i will put you in a support group
you could
make an acronym with your names
design t-shirts
laugh at the words i wrote about you
put the puzzle pieces together if
you can't figure out who i belonged to
at which point in time
i will put you in a support group
you could
meet every thursday
eat stale doughnuts
try to forget about me
but none of these men ever show up on time
and you always left early

when you
were standing right
beside me could you feel
the galaxy i put between us

i have been let down
by men
so many times

there is no disappointment left for you

i just want a brick by brick love story
please, men:
where's the concrete
foundation where you know
what you're looking for
and i know i'm it
all we've got are
leaky water beds
my knees are soaked from trying
to balance your instability
the sopping wet floor where
you left your promises to drown
is bound to cave in
give me cement
i'm tired of picking feathers out
from between my teeth
so here i sit
in barren land with dirt-stained knees
don't plant seeds of commitment
in my mind
if you never intend to water them

i tried so hard
to be whole for you
but it turns out

you like me better when i'm in pieces

i knew everything about who
i wanted you to be

and nothing about who you really were

i am having a funeral for
all the texts you typed
then deleted before
sending me

here lies
i know
poignant but too dramatic
it will be missed regardless

here lies
a rambling message
that goes on longer than
you have reached the maximum number of characters

here lies
i wish you said something
that one i'll kiss before covering it with dirt
cause it's what i wanted to read
but never will

here lies
you're crazy and i'm a narcissist
and honestly i can't close the casket on that one
because although i prefer *dramatic*
i know that it's true

i swear i would
stop thinking about you
but i know

you'll just come back when i do

since you left
i got worse at parallel parking
but i can drink coffee black
without making a face
i learned that it's possible
to not kill plants
and that i look best in
the mornings wearing
olive green
i've figured out how to ask
for what i want
to yell when i'm being talked over
that i can make people feel
things they've been ignoring
just by being honest
if i'm being honest
i still let myself think of you
once a day
and i will keep asking
even if you never hear me
can you let go of someone
without forgetting how they made you feel?

can you let go of someone
WITHOUT
FORGETTING
HOW THEY
MADE YOU
FEEL?

loving you was like
choosing to cross the tracks

even though i knew a train was coming

my love for you
won't leave
this city

the worst thing about loving you
wasn't you leaving

it was hoping you'd come back

the leftover
bits of my heart are crying out
no service
i am so sorry to disappoint but
you will not find
what you're looking for here

when he says that he's
scared of hurting you

it's not empathy, it's a warning

i am no longer soft
i built this city on
broken spines
and cracked open rib cages
my collar bones
prop up street lamps
femurs line railroads
tibias stacked to build straw homes
my smashed skull is why
no one lives here anymore
i am sorry you expected
petals when
all i'll ever have
are bones

i hope you don't mind
but i changed the lock on the door to my dreams
from now on no longer will you be able
to stare longingly at me from across tables
not saying a word
while my eyes are closed
even worse sometimes the pictures in my mind
play scenes of you pretending i no longer exist
though i am not awake
when you ignore me
it still brings tears to eyes shut
sometimes the story is wrapped around
you coming back
but even while asleep you manage
to make me so furious
with your purposefully
opposing opinions and
manipulative world views
as i lay here with this new dream lock i wonder
how does my unconscious know all the songs
you would have sang if you had never left
though this time there is a deadbolt
and i will not be making copies of the key

i thought
i would have a lifetime
to be in love with you

it ended in a second

if you fall in love
with someone's potential
you will break your own heart

this is me,
palms open, face up
asking for saving
this is me,
blue lips, bare skin
screaming in silence
this is me,
no brick in hand
no more wars left to fight
this is me,
hand on heart
this is me,
i am here
i am all that's left
this is me,
missing you

i held my breath
waiting for you
turns out i don't need you

i just need room to breathe

i am bursting at
my seams with joy
do you hear that?
it is the sound of
happiness
seeping out of me
but the ghosts around here
cast shadows of sadness
loneliness
i just want someone
to be happy with

i'm sorry
you were afraid
of my kind of love

things i can't let go of:

1. bad blood
2. missed birthdays
3. messages left on read
4. hangnails
5. makeup that's passed its prime
6. carbs
7. my first stuffed toy
8. the fear of falling
9. the fear of failing
10. split ends
11. empty wine bottles with nice labels
12. my mother's sweatshirt
13. pajamas with holes in them
14. checking a bag at the airport
15. writing everything in lowercase
16. black winged eyeliner
17. the number eighteen
18. you

your roots will always show you
the importance of holding on
to what grounds you
but don't ignore the lessons
the leaves are trying to teach you

i have let go of you
more than one thousand times
still you are a wave
always crashing back into me
i will keep floating
i will keep letting go
i will keep hoping
that this time is the last

ouroboros

[oor-uh-bohr-uhs]
noun

1. a circular symbol depicting a snake biting, swallowing, or eating its own tail, as an emblem of the cyclic nature of the universe: creation out of destruction.

don't cry at mavis and britannia
it took more than an intersection
for you to learn that red means it's over
and more than a white lie phone call
of i'll be there in fifteen
which still means thirty or an hour

when you are fed infidelity
you learn to be a prong
on the wheel of misfortune
you never learn how to build
a foundation
or a lasting bond between two

but you sure know
the step-by-step instructions
of breaking one down
i am dynamite
i am red means go
i am the collision

if i stay in the same place
how will i know
if you're leaving me
or just leaving

shh
don't say a word
i'm here to project all
my expectations onto you

google search, 'why am i only attracted to'

why am i only attracted to older guys
why am i only attracted to emotionally unavailable guys
why am i only attracted to my ex
why am i only attracted to guys in relationships
why am i only attracted to sociopaths

how is your timing
so bad

you'd think you'd never seen a clock

Why do we keep _LOVING_ people who can't _LOVE_ us back?

why is emotionally unavailable
typed under boyfriend material
in the dictionary i store the
broken pieces of my heart in
when did my brain learn that
crossed arms mean welcome home
if he tells you he doesn't text girls back
(it's not a joke)
he means it

how do commitment issues still send
a tingle down my spine
never been in a long-term relationship
translates into a challenge i can handle
him leaving at the crack of dawn feels
like a responsible decision
when it's all you've known
changing the subject when i ask about his mother
is just an inside joke between the two of us

i've learned to love the empty space
beside me in bed
but when i look at it long enough
i swear i can hear the outline
of where he used to lay ask me,
why do we keep loving people
who can't love us back?

some loves are not rational. they are simply impractical. they are not forever loves. they are fleeting moments. outstretched hands. a kiss on the cheek on tippy toes. they are falling asleep with the tv on, shoulders touching. they are voicemails that will never be listened to. a message that will never be read. but the great loves are not the only ones that help you grow. the little loves teach us how to love without expectation. the little loves teach us how to live a life filled with the love we deserve.

please don't look at me
this is not love
this is every breath i've ever taken
this is the north star
the sun rising until it bursts
this is more than my heart
this is i am in love with you
and i can't do anything about it

you make me feel
like myself
times infinity

build me a house
of LEGO
i need walls
that are easier to take down

i have been saving
this empty space for you

everyone else falls right through it

darkness falls so quickly
i can count down the
seconds until the sun sets
you, my dear, are not
so predictable
at eleven pm i listen
to the wind to see
if i can hear you
all i'm greeted with
is silence and my own
heart beat but
i will keep saving the
moon for you even
if there's no room for
me before midnight

i don't want to get
out of the water
i have grown accustomed
to being consumed by you
and even though
the moon tells me
it's time
i don't think i'll ever
be able to walk
on land again

it's just you,
me, and
blue morning light

i don't care
how we got here
i just want to scream
from rooftops with you

i can't explain where
all my love for you
came from
it's as if we once
raised a child
baby fingers gripping pinkies
or died together on
a bed of dandelions
it's as if i were the moon
and you were the sun
always convincing each other
the next day was worth rising for
and when i was too caught
up in being the ocean you
never forgot to remind me
what your earth felt like
i don't know if we'll finally
collide in this century
but i am certain i have
loved you in more than
a thousand different lifetimes

it's ok
to choose
to need someone

i cannot promise
how i will feel
tomorrow but
tonight i am in
love with you

fickle

i just want to
watch space jam
with you
talk about how
young michael jordan is
what is he even doing now
and how do the aliens
get so big i barely
remember the plot
of this but
something about
90s movies makes
me want to be with you

i wrote this on a sticky note
hoping it would turn into a permanent promise
we can just be bedhead and tea in the morning
if you wake up on the wrong side
i can be a smile that tries anyway
we can just be you and me hand in hand walking nowhere
laughing hard at nothing with no plans of stopping
we can just be car rides where i ask you to drive
if you let me change the station
i'll let you keep the windows open
we can just be the best and worst things
that have happened to each other
we can just be broken pieces glued together
we can just be north star and full moon
we can just be your trust and my fear of letting go
you can just be you
and i can just be me
and we can just be us

i keep seeing rainbows
that aren't there
baby, it's just droplets
reflecting in your eyes
cause these clouds are grey
and there's a sixty percent chance
it will still be raining
at midnight

there's something about
banter the quick back and
forth of a witty exchange
synchronicity at it's best
you can feel the tension
building up inside you
because girl, words
have always affected
you in ways hands can't
but the problem with
banter when it's typed is it's
said with no inflection left
to interpretation by
two people who have a
map but don't know where
they're going when you
decide to place your
black mirrors face down
and face each other
it can be hard for
your tongues to
speak the same language
of quick wit which your
fingers have memorized

you can have all
of me or
nothing at all

choose

how many times in the average day
do you think of me
while you're with her
and brush the thought away

where is she
while you're with me

where is she
while you're with me

where is she
while you're with me

is this what you wanted?

is This
what i
WANTED?

how many times will i let myself be
a second choice
before i learn that

there are no runner-ups in love

i feel prettier in the sun
warm me up
i need nose freckles
to feel like myself
hold my hand
before it melts
tell me i'm prettier
when it's warmer
tell me i'm prettier
than her

instead of treating people like possessions
i'm trying to treat them like
just-mine-for-a-while
a borrowed suitcase
or a hand-me-down sweater
i never know when i'll have to give you back
and you cannot be mine
if you belong to someone else

feelings
are
not
facts

therapy lessons part 2

three times
three times
three times
i've written this three times

a joint bank account
an engagement ring
a wedding
none of which
are signals

that it's my turn
it's not my turn
it's not my turn
it's not my turn

but still i crawl on the line
between friends and more than
all i've learned is how to love
in spaces that aren't mine
i'm holding on to smashed bricks
trying to build a foundation
from someone else's home

why did he look at me like that
why did he look at me like that
why did he look at me like that
why do you look at me like that

why do i keep falling in love
with people who are meant
for someone else

where do i find a man
who does not
want me to wait for him

if he's afraid to fully
fall in love with you

save your time and love yourself instead

you will always
be happy to see me
but never enough to stay

i don't know how to colour inside the lines
and it might be too late for me to learn
so i'm drawing maps
with convoluted directions
and i'm lost
and i'm ripping out the pages
and making them into paper airplanes
and i'm throwing them at your head
and i'm missing
and you don't see them
and i miss you
and you don't see me
and you're not leaving her
and you're not leaving her
and you're not leaving her

i have dedicated each of my bones
to an unworthy man
(crack, break)
here i am
once again in pieces
when will i learn that no man
needs to consume a part of me
and i have more to offer than just flesh

not everyone deserves
to hold your heart
in their hands

if he was worth waiting for
he would be with you now

you
can make
someone love
you but you can't
make them choose you

when we first met light reflected
between the two of us
laughter bonded our souls
oh, what a warm, easy love
things were so simple when
we didn't know what was
in store for us if only
i could have lived
in the clouds forever
with your lightning eyes
and raindrop lips
it's too bad gravity
took hold of us because
your heart is the only place
that has ever felt like home

you deserve a call me anytime love. a pick you up from the airport love. a love note on napkins kind of love. a chicken noodle soup for sore throats kind of love. a back rub before bed kind of love. a laughs at your bad jokes kind of love. a reminder to get up ten minutes earlier because it snowed and you're going to have to clean off your car kind of love. a clean off your car for you kind of love. a bring you cheesecake when you have cramps kind of love. a listening love. a love that takes care of you. a love that sees your messy hair, your morning breath, your spiralling mind, your no sleep crankiness, a love that loves you more because of it. you deserve a requited love. a love that lasts.

i've always been cyclical
good at returning to the start
bad at forgetting
these spirals won't spin themselves
i am so used to the
coming and going
the leaving
goodbye feels like the only thing i can rely on
but you
you have refused to be part of my cycles
there you are standing still
reliability looks so good on you
but you
you are a pillar meant to hold up someone else
and i can barely stand it
maybe it is time to get up
maybe it is time to move on
maybe this time
goodbye is meant for me

letting go

[let-ting goh]
verb

1. to stop holding something
2. to relax one's hold: release
3. to discuss or consider no further
4. often used figuratively: you need to let go of the past

when what you love loses meaning
life feels like swallowing lava
am i still breathing?
reading a book like
pouring acid into my eyes
how can i find kinship with printed words
when my sockets are sizzling flesh
when i dance my feet turn into
one hundred pound bags of sand
anchored with bones
what happened to cloud nine?
laughter like
shovelling coal into once red lungs
can you see the soot between my teeth?
i am coughing on black powder
but when i write
the ocean fills up my eyes
i am reminded that salt is healing
and words hurt less with eyes closed
one, two,
just breathe
three, four,
inhale, exhale
five, six
your life is worth so much more than this

you don't have to ignore
all the things
that you're sad about

am i depressed
am i depressed
am i depressed

i think i'm depressed
i think i'm depressed
i think i'm depressed

i'm depressed
i'm depressed
i'm depressed

nothing can change until you say it

what does it mean to feel like yourself

some days
self love is fragile
especially in
the bathroom mirror
if you pat yourself on the back
it doesn't count
if it's a fat hand
okay okay,
you got this
look at your reflection
i am worth it
look at your stomach
i am not
turn off the lights
skinny mary
skinny mary
skinny mary
all that appears
are the dimples on your arms
i just want to see
the hollows of my cheeks
some days are
tougher than others
when self love can't be
summoned from the outside in

i like to use the version of men
that only exists in my head
to fill the holes where otherwise

i feel nothing

michaela angemeer

spring smells like spruce
trees chopped down
outside my
three-story apartment
but i have more than three stories
to tell and
i am tired of being
the tree that everyone hangs from
(chop me down)
my limbs are getting sore
(chop me down)
my limbs are breaking off
(chop me down)
get it over with
i can't learn to stand on my own
without starting from nothing

i am just beginning

this year was the unpacking of all my baggage
no pocket left unturned
these zippers won't close anymore
i ripped them open
who knew you could fit all of this luggage
inside a cracked heart
this year i let go of
twenty-five years of worn-in leather
and scuffed nylon
did you see me explode?
i thought a backpack could hold
the doubts i had about my self-worth
turns out a duffel bag couldn't hide
my confused body image
my purse can hold three lipsticks
hand lotion
and a hair brush
but it's a little too small for all the horrible
things i've said about myself
and i never found
a suitcase big enough
to carry all the things i'm still afraid of
but i've realized that an open heart
can carry more than a cargo hold
and the palms of my hands are
so much warmer when held
by someone else
if i tie my hair with kindness and
sprinkle hope on my tongue

i can burn all of these suitcases
because i don't need to hide
what's inside myself
from anyone anymore

all you need to do
is take one step forward
your heart is growing stronger every day

you contain multitudes of love

You
contain
MULTITUDES
of
love

give yourself time
to let him go

it will happen slowly, then all at once

oh little honey–
i know today feels lonely
just take a deep breath
okay, one more

my sweet sweetheart–
at the end of the night
i know it feels like
all you have are these two hands
all i have are two hands
but don't you see how these hands can lift
they can hold you up
they can reach out
they can warm a cold heart
they can warm your cold heart

my darling baby girl–
don't you know that
you are a star in a beautiful galaxy
the moon will always wait for you
she's ready to teach you that
you can learn to feel connected
even when you are alone

and just like
the new moon
you will rebuild

you will become whole again

i don't know
what it's like
to be a damsel
in distress

i saved myself from you

remember,
you are infinite
with or
without him

he may have
felt like home
but he'll never
keep you warm at night

how did we become
a generation of women
who were told we need a man to be whole
without any role models
who are even worthy enough
to be our halves

my favourite women are travellers
nomads holding keys between their teeth
no baggage
ask them where they're going
they'll say
where the wind takes me
ask them when they're coming back
they'll smile
and you'll realize that
they never really leave

nobody is worth
letting go of your
self worth

when you leave a woman. light her hair on fire.
watch as her ashes litter the ground. you expect
her to blow into nothing when you walk away.
but you forget that women were made to burn.
women were made to rise again. a phoenix born
from ashes. one look, and you'll become dust.

i have no scrapes or bruises
my knees have not hit
earth in years i avoid
mountains as if they're
impossible to climb
i always walk around
instead of jumping over
i'd rather turn back than leap
but i'm learning that
if you want to find
love you have to be
willing to fall sometimes

there is a map to get to know me
i drew it in invisible ink
that you'll swear you can see
after a glass or two of red wine
this map has no end or beginning
just directions of me wanting
to get to know you
it'll never tell you which way is north
for my internal compass is too affected
by magnets and whatever direction
the moon wants to pull me in
it's less of a map and more of a dance
scattered drunk footprints
that think they're making their way somewhere
this map is too afraid to tell you who i am
though every day i will try to let you unfold it
but all i can manage right now
is to rip off this corner
lean closer so you can hear me
i think
just maybe
i'm learning that
you can share yourself
without losing pieces of you

i fell asleep on a sailboat
and woke up during
nautical twilight
but the stars were tired
of navigating
and i was tired of
being told what to do
they spit reflections
into the sea
and the waves spit back
sea spray whispered,
hold on tightly in my left ear
and *let go* in my right
so there i was
on salt-washed deck
holding on to what has
always been mine
and letting go of what
never belonged to me
in the first place

when i stopped looking
for love in someone else

i found love within myself

maybe i like boys
with broad shoulders
and thick necks
maybe i like girls
with long eyelashes
and upturned noses
but mostly
maybe i just like people
with warm hands
loud laughs
and good hearts

you
are always
worth fighting for

whatever's weighing
on your heart
baby,
let it go

it's ok to just be happy

It's ok to just BE HAPPY

your strength can
move mountains,
open hearts
if you let it

sometimes we forget how powerful we are

when is the last time
you told yourself
you are enough

i am the
only one who
can complete myself

this is the end of
the weeping. the
breaking. the cracking
myself in two. if i give
away any more pieces
i will cease to exist.
this is my promise.

i will be stronger this time

how hard it is to chisel these bricks
this room was not made for escaping
i do not need bars
i have no windows
(there is no oxygen left)
look at all these walls i've built
(count the bricks, i dare you)
have you ever tried to
demolish insecurity?
we need more than
a sledgehammer here
can't you see?

there is strength within vulnerability

when the future
feels far off
and you can't see
through the fog
don't forget to look for
right now,
right in front of you

he can't crawl his way
back into your life
if you're living
and loving above ground

i don't need a love
that sweeps me
off my feet

i need a love that tends to my roots

You'll find someone new, and someone new will find you

when your feet are heavier
than the concrete poured into sidewalks
and your pockets are filled with breadcrumbs
each step forward feels like you
are creating a destination out of anthills
formed on gaps and dandelions breaking dirt
you are forging a path
perhaps without end
but all you can do is put one foot forward
drop the breadcrumbs behind you
you'll find that the right person picks them up
no questions as to why you're leaving them
when they find your path
and finally find you
they'll see light feet and brightness
you are dancing in the fountain
look at how you shine
but today they still have breadcrumbs to collect
and you have a few more heavy steps to walk
but tomorrow,
tomorrow
you'll find someone new
and someone new will find you

start opening up your heart
to people
who are good for it

i am shining.
there are a million beads of light.
where did all this light come from?
who kept turning it off?
and how did i go so long without feeling happy?

you'll come back to yourself

acknowledgements

to my mother, thank you for teaching me that women can always find the strength to rebuild. to my father, thank you for buying twenty copies of *when he leaves you* and keeping them in your car to give to family at both awkward and endearing moments. to my brother, jacob, thank you for your continued belief in me and for doing my taxes. to my oma, thank you for your honest inquiry into my writing process and for your endless support. to chinye, cynthia, and michelle, thank you for your continued patience and love as i attempt to break my cycles and truly come back to myself. to aleks, thank you for your creative energy and for collaborating on the beautiful art that made its way into this collection, with a newborn in tow. to my readers, thank you for making me feel like i'm not alone. you give my writing so much more meaning than you know. and to everyone who continues to cycle their way in and out of my life. thank you for inspiring me to write this book.

about the author

michaela angemeer is a canadian poet who grew up in brampton, ontario. she went to the university of waterloo to pursue her love of introspection and words, receiving her bachelor of arts in psychology and english.

in 2018, michaela self-published her first collection of poetry, *when he leaves you*. the book debuted as the #1 new release in canadian poetry on amazon. her second book, *you'll come back to yourself,* is a collection of poetry and prose inspired by modern dating and broken relationships. it explores themes of lost love, infidelity, and learning to choose yourself.

michaela now lives in a one-bedroom apartment in waterloo, ontario with her frenchton, beatrice, her books, too many throw pillows, and bottles of red wine.

find her online:
michaelapoetry.com
@michaelapoetry